W9-BWF-435

DATE DUE

Published by Creative Education
123 South Broad Street, Mankato, Minnesota 56001
Creative Education is an imprint of The Creative Company

Designed by Stephanie Blumenthal

Photographs by James Blank, Don Eastman, Bob Ecker, Image Finders (Bachman,
Mark Gibson, Jefkin/Elnekave, Bruce Leighty), Gunter Marx, Richard Nowitz,
Photri, Tom Till, Unicorn Stock Photos (Andre Jenny), Marylin Wynn

Library of Congress Cataloging-in-Publication Data

McCrae, John (John R.).
Roads / by John McCrae.
p. cm. — (Designing the future)
Includes index.
ISBN 1-58341-188-7
1. Roads—History—Juvenile literature.
[1. Roads.] I. Title. II. Series.
TE149 .M25   2001
388.1'09—dc21   00-064471

First Edition

9 8 7 6 5 4 3 2 1

Cover, California desert highway; p. 1, road sign;
p. 2, road along California's Big Sur coastline;
p. 3, "curved road ahead" sign

ROADS

JOHN McCRAE

CREATIVE EDUCATION

Today, we have so many roads that it's easy to take them for granted. Yet, we depend on these roads to take us to many different places. Roads take us to work, to the library, to friends' houses. Roads provide access to natural resources such as iron ore, copper, diamonds, and gold. Roads bring food, clothing, and other products to our cities and towns. Roads take us to the shops and stores where we buy these items.

It's possible to drive on hundreds and thousands of miles of road. It's possible to drive on the

Highway along the Alaska Mountain Range

The Trans-Canada Highway

Before this extensive system of roads, people had to use other means of transportation. One of those means was water: the oceans, rivers, and lakes that form natural byways. People have been using waterways to travel for thousands of years. This is why so many cities are located on the ocean's coasts and the banks of rivers and lakes.

Sometimes, however, it is necessary to go places where there is no water route. One way to do this is to charge straight ahead, trying to knock away everything in the path. Another way is to follow the paths that animals and people have already made. Following an existing path is usually much easier, and is one of the oldest ways to build a road.

Trans-Canada Highway all the way from British Columbia to Nova Scotia. It's possible to drive north on the Alaska Highway to Fairbanks, Alaska. From there, it's even possible to drive south through Canada, the United States, and Mexico all the way to the southern part of Chile. But it hasn't always been this way.

The Trans-Canada Highway stretches about 5,000 miles (8,000 km) across Canada and links the 10 provinces. Officially opened in 1962, it runs from Victoria in British Columbia to St. John's in Newfoundland.

Old road through the Smoky Mountains

Petroglyphs mark an ancient Native American trail

When European settlers arrived in North America, they initially settled along the Atlantic Coast, near rivers and harbors. Later, when they moved inland, they discovered that the Native Americans had already created a system of trails. These trails followed the natural lay of the land and were frequently wide enough for only one person.

The Europeans used these same trails and soon widened them to make room for horses, wagons, and carriages. Many roads today follow the paths of these old trails. Broadway, the famous theater street in New York, for example, runs at an angle to the rest of the city's streets because it follows the route of an old Native American trail.

The Romans are the best known ancient road

The Royal Road was a path that connected the Spanish missions along the California coast in the 1700s. The missions were spaced so a person could walk from one mission to the next in one day. Today, U.S. Route 101 follows part of this road.

builders. Two thousand years ago, they maintained an Empire that stretched from England to Egypt and from Turkey to Spain. The Romans built roads to keep their empire connected. The expression "All roads lead to Rome" comes from this historical reality. The Romans constructed more than 53,000 miles (85,000 km) of roads.

A 2,000-year-old Roman road

Road through the ancient city of Pompeii, Italy

Roman roads were extraordinary examples of planning and engineering. The main reason the Romans were able to construct such solid roads was that they emphasized the preparation of the base. They placed layers of small stones in a trench, then added gravel in clay and tightly compacted stones bound with mortar. They packed down each layer and laid massive stone blocks over this base.

Roman roads were higher in the middle so rain would run off into ditches, which were dug on the sides.

Instead of following the natural slope of the land, Roman roads went straight from one point to the next. They were so well constructed that hundreds of years later people were still using them. One of these

Timbuktu became a prominent trading center in the 14th century because it was the meeting place of important roads. Camel caravans crossed the Sahara Desert on roads of shifting sand, carrying goods from North Africa. These goods were traded in Timbuktu for the products of the forests and grasslands of West Africa.

A camel caravan in West Africa

Travelers on the ancient Silk Road

roads, the Appian Way, runs southeast from Rome to Brindisi, on the Adriatic coast. Construction began in 312 B.C. under the supervision of Appius Claudius Caecus, a Roman official, and the completed road was named in his honor. Even today, many straight European roads are built upon the beds of ancient Roman roads.

Another famous ancient road was the Silk Road, which connected two major empires—Rome in the west and China in the east. It was more than 6,000 miles (9,600 km) long and crossed parts of what are now Turkestan, India, Iran, and China. More than 2,000 years ago, merchants used this route to trade gold and silver from Europe for valuable silks in China. This is the route

Runners used Native American trails to deliver messages between tribes. Some messengers could cover as many as 100 miles in a day on these trails.

Many mountain roads in Switzerland are built upon ancient paths

A 3,000-year-old stone road in Central America

that the Italian explorer Marco Polo used when he traveled to China in the 13th century.

In the New World, one of the most spectacular ancient roads was the Royal Road of the Incas in South America. The road was constructed of stones that fit together so tightly that they didn't need mortar. It ran 3,250 miles (5,230 km) along the highlands of the Andes Mountains. A second major road ran parallel with it along the coast, and these two roads were connected by other roads at important points. Using these roads, a team of relay runners could transport fresh fish all the way from the ocean to Cuzco, in the highlands, in only two days.

Just as ancient roads were built to meet the transportation needs of the times, roads in the original 13 colonies—and later the United States—were built to meet people's changing needs. In the 18th century, as more Europeans poured into the country, the East Coast became more heavily populated. Pressure to move west increased, and this westward expansion into Native American lands was led by men such as Daniel Boone.

In 1769, Daniel Boone headed west from North Carolina with a party of five men to find a route to Kentucky, a land rumored to be full of buffalo, deer, and wild turkeys. The group found the Warrior's Path, a trail used by Native Americans for hundreds of years, which crossed the Cumberland Mountains at the Cumberland Gap and continued into Kentucky.

Six years later, Boone and 30 well-equipped woodsmen expanded the trail. They used the existing trail, as well as buffalo trails, and in some places made

Modern-day roads crossing the Cumberland Gap

their own trails. They did this by making hatchet marks, known as blazes, on the trees to show the way. Because of this, they were called trailblazers, and the trail Boone blazed was called the Wilderness Road. By 1800, more than 200,000 settlers had used this road to travel into Kentucky.

Later, this trail was widened so that wagons could cross the mountains at the Cumberland Gap. As more settlers rushed west, other trails, also called traces, were expanded and became heavily traveled.

The Cumberland Gap National Historic Park

Covered wagons on the Oregon Trail

These included Zane's Trace into Ohio; the Natchez Trace from Nashville, Tennessee, to Natchez, Mississippi; and later the great trails that headed west from the Mississippi River: the Oregon Trail, the Santa Fe Trail, the Mormon Trail, and the California Trail.

Back east, more people were using carts, wagons, and carriages, but no national system of road building existed, so private individuals built roads and charged travelers fees to use them. The first extensive, hard-surfaced road in the United States was the Lancaster Turnpike, which opened in 1794. This toll road ran for 62 miles (100 km) from Philadelphia to Lancaster, Pennsylvania. In contrast to the dirt roads of the time, which became

John McAdam (1756–1836) was a Scottish engineer who developed a road surface made of small stones packed into layers over dry, prepared soil. This provided a smooth, durable surface for carriage and wagon traffic and was adopted extensively in Europe and America in the 19th century.

very muddy in wet weather, the Lancaster Turnpike was built of crushed rock and gravel. The road was wide enough to allow two lanes of wagon traffic and became a model for future roads.

In modern times, the development and spread of the automobile has had an enormous impact on road building. In the 20th century, as automobiles gained in popularity, drivers demanded more and better roads. Roads that had been designed to move peo-

R O A D   N A M E S

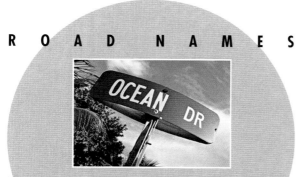

The naming of roads and streets reflects local interests. Mexico City, for example, has more than 200 streets with the name Cinco de Mayo (Fifth of May, a national holiday). A road's geographic location may also influence its name.

Old country road in Illinois built with crushed rock

Gravel road running through Ohio woodlands

ple, animals, and wagons then had to be widened and upgraded for cars. Dirt paths that had been good enough for horses were not acceptable to automobile drivers.

The biggest change brought about by the automobile, however, was in people's perception of distance. The automobile could travel much faster than a horse or a person on foot, and this changed people's sense of how far away things were. Rather than thinking of distance in miles, people began to think of distance in terms of time. If someone says that the store is fifteen minutes away, that probably means it's fifteen minutes away by car on a good road.

Karakorum Highway connects Pakistan and China through the Karakorum Mountains. The winding road climbs to the Khunjerab Pass, which is 15,748 feet (4,800 m) above sea level, making it one of the highest roads in the world.

Smooth blacktop roads make car travel faster

Streets in urban areas are often closely flanked by houses

As more people began to drive cars, the demand for roads increased. Likewise, once more roads were built, more people bought cars to use the roads that were so convenient. When these roads became crowded, people demanded still more roads. This cycle continues to the present day.

Building a modern road involves a number of steps. The first of these is planning. Local, regional, and national transportation officials assess what is needed at the moment and what will be needed in the future. They study where people live, where they work, where goods are made, where they're sold, and how all these things and people get where they need to go. Officials count the cars on the roads and decide whether to expand existing roads or build new ones.

In many countries, citizen involvement is an important aspect of planning. Meetings are held so that interested citizens can express their views on the

Natural obstructions can make road planning and construction difficult

Highway bridge to Richmond, Virginia

idea of rebuilding existing roads or building new ones. Officials and citizens discuss how much the new road will cost, how it will benefit people's lives, and what impact it will have on the environment.

Engineers develop designs for the new road. A modern road requires a large amount of land, called a right-of-way, to accommodate the road, the shoulders, and the ditches. Set backs, the areas beside the road, are also part of this right-of-way. To ensure that drivers will have a clear view of approaching traffic, nothing can be built in the set back area.

One of the biggest considerations in road building is water. Water flows along the easiest course to lower ground, and if a road isn't planned properly, it will wash out in a heavy rain. Because of this, engineers use culverts, big long tubes, to carry water under the road, and they build bridges to go over rivers and streams.

Once a plan has been chosen and all the proper governmental and legal permissions have been obtained, the next step is clearing the land. Cutting trees, removing stumps, blasting rock, and removing existing buildings may all be part of this process. When the clearing is complete, huge machines are brought in to begin construction.

Rather than follow the lay of the land, as past builders did, today's road crews are able to build almost anywhere. They use a cut-and-fill technique. Earth movers and bulldozers dig the dirt from the top of hills and dump it in low spots and valleys to make the road as even as possible. Graders smooth the surface. Sand, stone, and crushed rock are hauled in, dumped, and packed down to make the base of the road as durable as possible.

A mountain road built using a cut-and-fill technique

An elevated highway made of cement concrete

The road is now ready to be paved. One modern pavement surface is portland cement concrete, a mixture of sand, water, crushed stone, and portland cement, which is a heated combination of limestone and clay. Another modern surface is bituminous pavement, also called blacktop. This is made by mixing sand, gravel, and crushed stone with bitumens, which are asphalts and tars. Whichever surface is used, it is laid down by a paving machine.

Once the surface sets, lights, traffic signs, and road markers are installed. These road markers look very different from the blazes that marked earlier trails, but their purpose is the same: to mark the route. Finally, the planners, engineers, and inspectors check to make sure everything is up to standard. If it is, the road is ready for people to use.

One way to see the automobile's impact on road construction is to compare maps of an old city

A highway snaking through hilly terrain

A Philadelphia highway aglow with car lights

with a modern one. The old city has narrow, winding streets that were built for people on foot or with carts. The modern city has long, straight roads and freeways that were designed to move cars quickly.

Another way to see the automobile's impact on our lives is to contrast maps of places that still have relatively few roads with places that have many. Northern Canada, the interior of Australia, northern Russia, and parts of central Congo still contain large

H I G H W A Y S

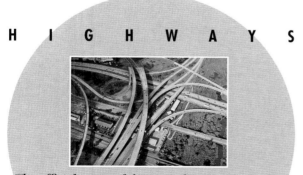

The official name of the United States' network of interstate highways is the Dwight D. Eisenhower System of Interstate and Defense Highways. It contains more than 45,000 miles (72,000 km) of roads that crisscross the United States.

Street congestion in New York City

Coastal roadway in Santa Cruz, California

Gravel road in the sparsely populated Canadian Yukon

areas without roads. In contrast, hundreds of roads fan out from major cities like the spokes on a bicycle wheel, linking the cities with small towns and other cities. The number of roads reflects the number of people in an area and their need to get to and from other places.

Just as it would have been difficult 100 years ago to imagine what our roads would look like today, it is difficult today to imagine what they'll look like 100 years from now. Maybe our roads will become increasingly crowded and the demand for more roads will increase. Maybe our use of other forms of transportation—such as trains, planes, and boats—will increase. It's also possible that new forms of transportation that we haven't yet imagined will emerge. Whatever happens, we'll continue to need some form of road to connect us to the people we want to see and the places we want to go.

I N D E X